A CHURCH LEADER'S GUIDE TO CHILD DEDICATION AND YOUTH BAPTISM

by David Michael

Truth:78

A Church Leader's Guide to Child Dedication and Youth Baptism
By David Michael

Our vision at Truth78 is that the next generations know, honor, and treasure God, setting their hope in Christ alone, so that they will live as faithful disciples for the glory of God. Our mission is to inspire and equip the church and the home for the comprehensive discipleship of the next generation.

We equip churches and parents by producing curricula for Sunday School, Midweek Bible, Intergenerational, Youth, and Backyard Bible Club settings; vision-casting and training resources (many available free on our website) for both the church and the home; materials and training to help parents in their role in discipling children; and the Fighter Verses™ Bible memory program to encourage the lifelong practice and love of Bible memory.

Copyright © 2022 Next Generation Resources, Inc. Illustrations Truth78. All rights reserved. No part of this publication may be reproduced in any form without written permission from Truth78.

Published in the United States of America by Truth78.

Scripture quotations are from the Holy Bible, English Standard Version® (ESV®), copyright © 2001 Crossway, a publishing ministry of Good News Publishers. ESV Text Edition: 2016. Used by permission. All rights reserved.

ISBN: 978-1-952783-61-6

Truth:78

Equipping the Next Generations to Know, Honor, and Treasure God

Truth78.org
info@Truth78.org
(877) 400-1414

Table of Contents

Introduction to the Guide 4
Part 1: Child Dedication 7
    Child Dedication Approach and Process 8
        Introduction. 8
        Secure Support from Church Leadership 9
        Promises to Remember. 9
        Preparing Parents for Dedication. 10
        The Dedication Service. 13
    Child Dedication Resources and Sample Documents 24
        Parental Promises for the Dedication of Children (in Question Format). 24
        Pastoral Pronouncement. 24
        Parental Promises and the Dedication of Children (with Explanation) 25
        Recommended Books. 28
        Pastor Instructions for Dedication Service 29
        Sample Prayer of Dedication. 37
        Sample Pastor Letter (to go inside the baton). 38
Part 2: Preparing Young People for Baptism. 41
    Youth Baptism Approach and Process. 42
        Introduction. 42
        Securing Support from Church Leadership 43
        Steps in the Process 44
        Pastoral Considerations 47
    Youth Baptism Resources and Sample Documents. 52
        Sample Proposal for a Revised Baptism Preparation Process 52
        Preparing Young People for Baptism and Church Membership:
        An Overview for Parents and Church Leaders 54
        Children and the Lord's Supper 58
        Frequently Asked Questions 62
        Youth Baptism Interview Team Packet 65
            Preparation for the Baptism/Member Interview: Interview Team Letter 65
            Suggested Questions for Youth Baptism/Membership Interview. 67
            Essential Elements of the Gospel 69
            The Meaning of Baptism. 74
        Pastor/Elder Questions and Response for the Baptism Service. 75

For more helpful resources, including PDF forms that you can customize, notes and outlines for the Parenting Foundation and Baptism Classes, and even video and audio links of dedication services, see Truth78.org/dedication-baptism-resources

Introduction to this Guide

To be trusted by God to raise His image bearers in the fear and joy of the Lord is an unspeakable privilege. Because parents and church leaders share this responsibility, it is important for there to be a true spirit of partnership and cooperation between the church and home.[1]

This guide is meant to be a companion to the booklets *Dedicated to the Lord* and *Established in the Faith*, both of which are available through Truth78.org. These two companion booklets outline the biblical principles and vision behind the dedication of children and, when the time is right, preparation for baptism. This information for child dedication and youth baptism is not only intended to help church leaders make the most of these milestones, but it is also intended to do this in a way that promotes partnership and maximizes the impact for all who are involved in the process.

Though there are other milestones, there is a uniqueness and connection between child dedication and baptism. The dedication of children anticipates their baptism. Parents dedicate their children in the hope that they will, as explained in *Dedicated to the Lord*, "belong wholly to Jesus Christ forever."[2] One of the promises that parents make is to regularly pray that, by God's grace, their child "will come to trust Jesus Christ alone for the forgiveness of his/her sins and for the fulfillment of all His promises to him/her, even eternal life and in this faith follow Jesus as Lord and obey His teachings."[3] This promise links to the questions the child will be asked when, Lord willing, he is baptized several years later: "Are you now trusting in Jesus Christ alone for the forgiveness of your sins and the fulfillment of all His promises to you, even eternal life?"[4] and "Do you intend, with God's help, to obey Jesus' teachings and to follow Him as your Lord?"[5]

---

[1] In pages 35-43 of the book, *Zealous: 7 Commitments for the Discipleship of the Next Generations* by David Michael, commitment #2 is "Foster a Robust Partnership Between Church and Home." This chapter provides the biblical foundation for the shared calling and responsibility of the church and home for the discipleship of the next generation. (This booklet is available through Truth78.org.)
[2] This is from the concluding words of the dedication on page 44 in *Dedicated to the Lord: Five Parental Promises for the Faithful Discipleship of Children.*
[3] Ibid., 38.
[4] This from the first of three questions that affirm faith in Christ on page 34 in *Established in the Faith: A Discipleship Guide for Discerning and Affirming a Young Person's Faith.*
[5] Ibid., 35 (from the second of the three questions).

As the title of this guide suggests, it has been prepared to serve church leaders who are responsible for planning and overseeing child dedication services and/or the baptism of young people. The content has been drawn from 23 years of experience in two different churches. In both churches, the dedication of children and preparation of young people for baptism were connected to and designed to reinforce the biblical vision for the discipleship of the next generation that we were pursuing in those churches.[6] Certainly, the preparation process, content of the instruction, communication, and service details should be adapted to fit the unique traditions and culture of each church. We are happy for these tools and various forms of communication to be adapted and used to effectively serve the church. May God bless your efforts for His glory and for the comprehensive discipleship and everlasting joy of the next generations.

---

6 This biblical vision for discipleship is unpacked in the book *Zealous:7 Commitments for the Discipleship of the Next Generation*.

PART 1: CHILD DEDICATION

Child Dedication Approach and Process

Introduction

In *Dedicated to the Lord*, a companion booklet to this guide, I stated that the "dedication of children is an act of faith in the presence of God and His people in which we solemnly and earnestly offer our children up to God for His wise and sovereign purposes in their lives, and offer ourselves up to God for the holy responsibility of being biblical parents and raising our children in the fear, knowledge, and joy of the Lord."[7] Though not mandated in Scripture, I want to commend the public dedication of children in the church and offer some practical guidance for the overseeing pastor or church leader.

Alongside the reasons and practical benefits given in *Dedicated to the Lord*,[8] the dedication service is an opportunity to promote a biblical vision for the next generation and to reinforce personal and corporate responsibility for the faithful and comprehensive discipleship of the children growing up in the church.

Although I wasn't the preaching pastor for the two churches I served, as a next-generation pastor with responsibility for child dedication services, I was assured of having the congregational ear for at least 10-15 minutes every three months. In planning each service, I wanted to make every second count for casting vision and calling for commitment from dedicating parents and from the congregation. In my experience, the dedication service, the parent preparation for it, and the follow-up afterward proved to be one of the most effective ways to inspire and impart a biblical understanding of next-generation ministry in the church.

---

7 This is from the working definition of child dedication on page 8 in *Dedicated to the Lord*.
8 Ibid., 10-11.

Secure Support from Church Leadership

Before taking steps to establish or revise a child dedication service in the church, it is wise to seek awareness, support, and perhaps official action from the elders and senior leadership of the church. There are at least four reasons why this is important.

1. Whether or not the five suggested promises are used, it is important for leaders to recognize and affirm whatever promises parents make as the biblical standard for parental and congregational responsibility for the children of the church.
2. It is important for elders to understand what child dedication is and its implications since, in most cases, dedicating parents along with the congregation will be accountable to the elders for keeping the promises they make.
3. It is also important for elders to understand the process and be aware of the communication, instruction, and materials that dedicating parents receive before and after a child is dedicated.
4. Making it an *official* action of the elders often helps to preserve the wording of the promises and, to some degree, the tone and format of the service for years and even generations to come.

Promises to Remember

The wording of the dedication promises, the pastoral pronouncement, and many of the service details are important and should be consistent from service to service. A church should settle on a service format and the wording for the promises they will ask parents to make and stick to them. This can seem rigid and inflexible but, in the long run, I believe it helps preserve the integrity of the service and the significance of the promises.

Dedication promises should be carefully crafted using precise language that can succinctly capture the essence of parental commitment. Preserving that language over time serves as a regular reminder to parents of the promises they made. In our 33 years at Bethlehem Baptist Church of Minneapolis, my wife Sally and I witnessed hundreds of parents dedicating their children and making the same exact promises that we made when we dedicated our daughters in 1982 and 1985. At each dedication service, Sally and I were reminded of the promises we made. Even though our daughters have no memory of their dedications, they grew up witnessing regular dedication services and thus were reminded of the pledge their mom and dad made to God and to the people of Bethlehem. When parents faced challenges in the various stages of parenting, we could remind each other, encourage each other, and support each other in keeping the promises we all made.

Preparing Parents for Dedication

Taking sufficient time to engage with parents and prepare them for dedicating their children is one of the most fruitful investments we can make. This reinforces the significance of the promises and encourages parents to consider them carefully.

It is also an opportunity to begin equipping parents for their most important responsibility. It has been my experience that many parents are out of touch with their responsibility for the discipleship of their children, and even more lack the understanding or tools they will need for the task before them. We have found that the time taken to lay a foundation for the parents' biblical responsibility can help encourage a deeper awareness of their God-given roles and provide more assurance of God's grace to help them in doing an otherwise impossible job.

Parenting Foundations Seminar

Within a month prior to each dedication service, we offered a seminar to parents planning to dedicate their children. Parents were encouraged to take the class before dedicating their first child and then, if they so desired, they could come back for a refresher prior to the dedication of subsequent children.

The class was structured around the five dedication promises. In the first hour, we covered promises one through three. In the second hour, dads and moms met separately to consider their unique roles and responsibilities in fulfilling the fourth promise. For the final hour, we came back together to cover promise five and the pastoral pronouncement.

The primary goal was to do all we could to help parents understand the implications of the promises they were making and offer them some guidance for how to keep them. We also used the time to lay the foundations for our parenting ministry and the discipleship of children and youth in the church. At Bethlehem, this seminar was the first in a series of four "Foundation Builder Seminars" that we offered to parents, each targeting children in different age ranges (0-2, 3-5, 6-9, and 10-12 years old). In each of these seminars, including this first one, we tried to answer three main questions: What can parents do at home to disciple children within the age range we were focused on? What do we do at church to disciple their children? In what ways can the church and parents partner together for the discipleship of their children?

We were aware that the pre-dedication might be the one and only opportunity we had to inspire, challenge, and instruct some of the parents. Over the years of working with parents, Sally and I learned that, in general, parents who voluntarily attend parenting classes and seminars are usually the ones who were the most teachable, the most conscientious, and the most eager to learn and grow as parents. Because dedicating parents were expected to attend this first class in the series, we were able to reach parents who otherwise might not attend.

At the end of the class, we often asked parents to complete a three-minute exit survey, which confirmed what we assumed—not everyone who attended the class wanted to be there, and some came feeling a bit irritated that they had to give up a Saturday morning just to dedicate their child. The survey also confirmed that most, if not all, of those same disgruntled parents were so glad they came and, by the end of the class, left humbled, sobered, challenged, inspired, and ready to pledge their faithfulness to the high and holy calling of parenting.

The substance of the material we presented in the class is contained in *Dedicated to the Lord*, one of the companion booklets for this guide. Parents who attended the class received a complimentary copy of the booklet for future reference and a reminder of what was covered in the class. Even though reading the booklet alone could provide adequate preparation for dedicating parents, this benefit is far outweighed by the benefits of being together in person and learning alongside other parents.

As a pastor of large churches, the class provided the opportunity for me to personally engage with parents, build trust, and open doors to ongoing ministry with them and their families. It gave me an opportunity to look parents in the eye and say, "We are with you in this!

When you stand before the congregation and make these promises, remember that you and your children are surrounded by brothers and sisters who love you and care about the outcome of your children's faith and, even if we fail, God will never fail you. He is for you and not against you. He is able to do for you and your children beyond what you ask or imagine."

During the second hour, while my wife and her co-teacher were meeting with the moms, my co-teacher and I were able to encourage and challenge fathers in their shepherding roles. I am persuaded that the key to effective and fruitful ministry to children and youth in the church is an effective and fruitful ministry to men. I wanted men to understand that the mantle of responsibility for keeping the dedication promises rests mainly on them. I also wanted to give them some principles to follow, suggest a few tools to help them, and, again, offer to support them along the way.

The class also provided the opportunity to help parents understand and embrace the vision, goals, and priorities for next-generation ministry in the church. We made sure to include children's discipleship staff, who explained how vision shaped our strategies and offered practical guidance and application for discipleship in the home. This served to invite connection between parents and ministry leaders on a few different levels.

Alternatives to the Class

When it was impossible for one or both parents to attend the class prior to the dedication, we offered some alternatives.

- The week before the dedication service, parents received a letter that provided details about the service, as well as a summary and explanation of each of the promises.
- Parents who could not attend the seminar were notified and encouraged to attend a future class. They were also offered an audio or video recording of a previous class and encouraged to listen to it prior to the service.
- Parents who missed the class were encouraged to read *Dedicated to the Lord* before the dedication service.
- During COVID-19, when the in-person class was not an option, we provided parents with a copy of *Dedicated to the Lord* ahead

of time and met with them on Zoom for an abbreviated class that covered the highlights and allowed for some discussion, questions, and personal connections.

- When available, livestreaming the session may also accommodate some situations.

Resources

One of the ways to serve parents is to point them to good resources that can help them in their discipleship efforts. Parents who attended the class received a resource kit that included not only *Dedicated to the Lord* but also some other books and resources recommended and provided by the church. (See the Recommended Books list in the Child Dedication Resources and Sample Documents section in this booklet.)

A Dream That Never Came True

A step in the dedication process that I was not able to implement was for the dedicating parents to receive a visit in their homes from one of the elders, either before the dedication or as a follow-up to it. The hope was that this would acquaint parents with at least one of their elders and open the door for ministry to the family. The elder could take the spiritual temperature of the home and discern if there were any needs or concerns in the marriage or family. It would also provide an opportunity to reinforce the seriousness and significance of the dedication promises, as well as affirm our commitment to support parents as they seek to raise their children in the fear and the joy of the Lord. (See the Elder Home Visit for Child Dedication form at Truth78.org/dedication-baptism-resources)

The Dedication Service

In preparing the dedication service, it is helpful to review the benefits and biblical rationale for including the dedication of children in the rhythm of corporate gathering in the local church.[9]

- It is good and fitting in the context of corporate worship to glorify God and praise Him for His amazing, person-forming

---

[9] See pages 7-11 of *Dedicated to the Lord* for more on the historical roots, the Bible's teaching, and the practical benefits of child dedication.

work and His gracious generosity and creative power (Psalm 111:1-2; Psalm 145:10-12).

- It is an opportunity for parents and the church to publicly acknowledge our children as gifts of God, to celebrate His blessing, and to give thanks to Him for these gifts (Job 1:21; Romans 11:34-36; Psalm 127:3).

- It is an act of surrender and submission to God and His will for our children, who were ultimately created for His glory and His purposes (Isaiah 43:6-7; Isaiah 46:9-11; Ephesians 1:3-4).

- It is a declaration of parental and congregational commitment to be examples of godliness and to raise our children in the fear, knowledge, and joy of the Lord (Deuteronomy 6:6-7, 20-21; Ephesians 6:4).

- It is a corporate appeal to God for His grace for the sake of our children in the hope that they will be in Christ, holy and blameless before the Lord (Ephesians 1:4) and belong wholly to Him forever (1 Thessalonians 4:17).

Additionally, we saw that the dedication service provides an opportunity to promote a biblical vision for the next generation and to reinforce personal and corporate responsibility for the faithful and comprehensive discipleship of the children growing up in the church.

The child dedication service should fit with the culture, tradition, style, and preferences of the church while being careful to preserve a dignity to the service with a tone that exalts the person-forming glory of God and reflects the solemnity of the promises being made.

Although there is something to be said for flexibility in planning the service, keep in mind the value of establishing the service as a tradition with a consistent format from service to service, year to year, and even generation to generation. As the years go by, the dedication service will become a regular reminder to those who previously dedicated a child of the promises they made and will kindle afresh the heartfelt desires that every Christian parent and grandparent has for their children.

The basic structure for the services I led included the following:

1. **Pastoral Tone-Setting Word of Introduction**

    This is a brief opportunity to link the dedication of children to a larger biblical vision for the next generation. It can be directed to the parents as a word of hope, challenge, or encouragement. It can also be directed to the congregation and reinforce their crucial role in support of the parents and the ministry to children and youth in the church.

2. **Parental Affirmation of Dedication Promises**

    This is the heart of the dedication service when parents make public their commitment to the dedication promises. At this point, the officiating pastor/elder/leader faces the dedicating parents and asks them to respond to each of the promises, stated as questions. Parents are instructed ahead of time to respond to the questions by saying "I do" (not "We do") since each parent is individually called to be faithful to the promises. It is helpful if the congregation can see as well as hear the promises being made—perhaps projected on a screen or printed in a service folder.

3. **Personal Introduction of Dedicating Parents and Children**

    This needs little explanation except to say it is usually something simple like "This is John and Mary Doe and their son (or their third child), John David." Depending on the time available, there may be a backstory to tell or something about the parents or child that would provide some helpful context for the congregation (such as an adoption, special birth story, etc.).

4. **Pronouncement**

    I recommend that these words, like the promises, be the same each time. I found it helpful to have the words memorized so that I could make close eye contact with the child and have my right hand free as I said:

    > *John David, together with your parents who love you dearly and this congregation that cares about the outcome of your faith, I dedicate you to God, surrendering together with them all worldly claims upon your life in the hope you will belong wholly to Jesus Christ, forever.*

At the end of the pronouncement, it was part of our tradition to say, "And all the people said amen!" Usually ahead of time we would alert the congregation that they would be invited to say "amen" as each child is dedicated. We explained that the amen is a corporate affirmation that "this congregation cares about the outcome of the child's faith," and it expresses each member's willingness to do all he can to support the parents and the faith and discipleship of the child.

5. **Presentation of Certificates, Symbols, Gifts, Etc.**

   Usually, churches want to mark the occasion by presenting parents with a certificate, gift, or symbol. At Bethlehem, after the words of dedication were pronounced, the parents were presented with a certificate of dedication and a long-stem, red rose. For decades, the red rose was a symbol of new life at Bethlehem. Whenever a child was born or adopted into a family in the church, the birth was celebrated and announced on Sunday with a red rose on the piano.

   At College Park, instead of a rose, there was a 20-plus-year tradition of presenting dedicating parents with a baton, symbolizing the passing of faith from one generation to the next. Inside the baton was a letter written by the pastor for the child to open and read on his 18th birthday. I loved this idea and had the privilege of developing this symbol into what became a time capsule of sorts. In addition to a pastoral letter, we included in the baton the promises that parents made, the prayer of the dedication that was prayed, a certificate with a text based on the benediction/blessing used in the service, and a list of the other children who were dedicated on that day. Parents received copies of everything inside so that the baton could remain sealed until the child's 18th birthday. (Visit Truth78.org/baton for information on purchasing a child dedication baton. See samples of what we included inside the baton at Truth78.org/dedication-baptism-resources)

6. **Prayer of Dedication and Blessing**

   For more than two decades, it has been an unspeakable privilege for me to conclude dozens of dedication services with a prayer that praises the Giver and Sustainer of Life and expresses the heart desires of the congregation and parents—not only for the children being dedicated but for the next generations as a whole. God used the time and effort to prepare these prayers to sustain in me and many others a God-centered zeal for the next generation to set their hope in God.

To help inspire such prayers for the next generation, I prepared a booklet entitled *Big, Bold, Biblical Prayers for the Next Generation* (available through Truth78.org). The booklet includes several sample prayers, most of which I prepared for child dedication services.

When stepping up to pray, consider inviting family and friends to come forward and gather around each family. Those who remain seated can be encouraged to extend their hands toward the families. This is a way for the church to participate in the prayer and to physically express support.

At the conclusion of the prayer, it was my custom to lift my hands above the parents and children, look at them, and pronounce a memorized blessing/benediction. For more on this and several biblical blessings/benedictions you can use, please refer to *A Father's Guide to Blessing His Children* (available through Truth78.org).

Special Circumstances for Service Planning

Single Parents

When preparing parents for dedication, it is important that we do not minimize the marriage as the foundation for the discipleship of children, along with the benefits to children who grow up in a functional, godly, two-parent home. However, on this side of heaven, through various circumstances, most of which are difficult and painful, there will be parents faced with the challenge of raising children without the benefit of a spouse. It is important for leaders to know who these parents are and for the leaders to go out of their way to encourage, support, equip, and pray for them. One of the best ways to begin expressing that support is in the dedication service.

Many single parents will loathe the thought of standing up in front of the church and calling attention to their situation. For some, just observing a dedication service can add to the isolation they feel in the church. Therefore, they will likely need encouragement and even a little gentle persuasion to participate in a dedication service, especially if they don't see other single parents dedicating their children.

As indicated elsewhere in this guide, there are some opportunities to offer hope and express support for single parents. However, for the most part, the single parent should be welcomed and treated like every other parent in the preparation process and on stage during the dedication service.

Several years ago, I presided over a dedication service that included a single mom. A few days later I received a letter from another single mom who had observed the service. With her permission, I am concluding this section with an excerpt from her letter. It provided helpful insight into the perspective and the heart of a single parent and opened my eyes to the impact that a child dedication service can have.

> *My husband left our family the day after Christmas and filed for divorce this past week. (I am still praying for a miracle to turn this nightmare around.) We have 2 children, ages 3 and 1. When I saw all the families coming on the stage this morning, I took a deep breath and prayed, "God help me get through this." I noticed the single woman standing on the stage with her son. I immediately prayed...that she would have strength standing there alone with her son. I have wanted to dedicate my kids but have never seen a single mom on the stage before and did not know how to even go about asking if that was even OK. I thought you all handled this morning's dedication so well. I noticed you were sensitive to her and did not even mention the importance of keeping the marriage together. My passion is for my children to follow Jesus one day, and dedication is important to me. And this morning showed me that it is OK to stand up there alone. Thank you for being loving to that woman. Thank you for not making it awkward. Thank you for supporting her decision to dedicate her son. It was powerful. God used it in my life. It was a reminder to me as well that I am not the only person raising children alone. I pray it also was used in others' lives, and they will see a need to come alongside her and encourage her as she points her son to Jesus...I am so thankful that I am in a church that has such a strong and genuine desire to reach the hearts of our children with Jesus.*

Multiple Children

It is not uncommon for parents to present more than one child for dedication. Often these are parents who are newer to the church and came from a church where dedication was not practiced. This is not a problem, but it is helpful to consider a couple of logistical questions.

Once the parents and the children are introduced, you can pronounce the words of dedication one at a time or all together ("John, Rebecca, and Elizabeth, together with your parents who love you dearly and this congregation, I dedicate you to God..."). If you are dedicating two children at a time, it works to put one hand on each child. If there were more than two, I moved one hand from child to child as I pronounced the words of dedication. My preference was to dedicate each child separately. The only reason for dedicating children together was because of the time constraints on the service.

Older Children

Technically there is no age limit for parents to dedicate their children, but I encouraged them to do this within the first two years of their child's life. I did not encourage parents to dedicate children older than age five unless they were being dedicated with younger siblings. It was not uncommon to see parents dedicating older children, but this was usually because they had younger children also being dedicated.

Other times, parents who come to see the value of dedicating children regret not doing it when their children were younger. Some may feel as though they have deprived their child of something important and want to make it right. We want to assure them that their children are not deprived of their parent's dedication if they are, indeed, dedicated to the calling that is implied by the five dedication promises. We want to help them be more focused on being intentional and faithful in the discipleship of their children.

Pastors/Elders and the Dedication of Their Own Children

One of joys that pastors and elders have is the opportunity to officiate some of the milestone events of their own children. Should a pastor/elder officiate the dedication of his own child? I would not recommend this in the same way I would not recommend a pastor officiating his own marriage ceremony. Because the parental promises are at the heart of the dedication service, it is important that the pastor identify more as a father than a pastor in that moment and demonstrate his commitment and accountability to the church for keeping the promises he makes. Therefore, it is best if another pastor or elder preside over the service. If there is a desire for the pastor to have a part in the service, it would certainly be fitting for him to pray the prayer of dedication or perhaps give the opening remarks.

Pastoral Questions to Consider

There are several questions that pastors and elders need to consider and be prepared to answer, including the following:

1. **Are parents being asked to make a promise or a vow?**

    In one sense, there is no significant difference between a promise and a vow. A vow is a promise, but it is a solemn promise often made before God and witnesses. At Bethlehem, we spoke of child dedication, alongside church membership and the marriage ceremony, as one of three occasions when we call people to make covenant commitments. Church leaders will need to decide if the parental promises should be elevated to that level.

2. **Should child dedication be limited to church members?**

    There are good and godly reasons on both sides of this question. Mutual submission, accountability, responsibility, and commitment often come with church membership. It can be difficult for the congregation to commit to supporting dedicating parents if those parents are not committed to being part of the church or submissive to the leadership. On the other hand, there will be parents who are active and committed participants who, for various (and sometimes good) reasons, are not members. Also, it can be argued that it is good and loving to give parents the opportunity to publicly thank God for the gift of a child and call them to parental faithfulness—even if they are not yet members. Elders will need to wrestle with this question and decide.

3. **Should unmarried parents who are living together dedicate their children?**

   Child dedication and the preparation for it can provide opportunities before and after the dedication to counsel and challenge parents in areas where they need to grow that we might otherwise not have. For this and other reasons, church leaders may decide to permit unmarried parents to dedicate their children. In both churches where I served, we declined this opportunity, believing that it is important for parents to embrace the wisdom of God's standards and model joyful submission to God's purpose for covenant commitment in marriage.

4. **Should a single parent dedicate a child?**

   Even if there is an obvious and definite yes to this question, it is important that elders address it and affirm it. As I explained in *Dedicated to the Lord,* "it is important to understand that we make the [dedication] promises as individuals. If our spouse dies, leaves the marriage, or shirks his or her responsibility, we are still called to be faithful parents."[10] The church must support all parents, especially single ones, given the extra challenges that a single parent may face in the effort to fulfill the dedication promises.

5. **Should unbelieving parents dedicate their children?**

   Although it might be good for elders to discuss this, it is difficult to imagine how people could honestly make these promises if they are not trusting Christ.

6. **Should a Christian parent dedicate the child if his/her spouse is not a believer?**

   It is fitting for a Christian parent whose spouse is not trusting Christ to dedicate a child, provided the unbelieving parent will not hinder the Christian parent's efforts to keep the dedication promises. To recognize a child as a gift of God and give heartfelt thanks for that gift (Promise #1) requires little if any support from a spouse. However, promising to bring up a child in the discipline and instruction of the Lord (Promise #3) would be

---

10 This is from a footnote on page 43 of *Dedicated to the Lord.*

difficult to make if the unbelieving parent was opposed. A Christian parent, ideally with a pastor/elder, should discuss the dedication, review the promises, and solicit the support of the unbelieving spouse. Elders may consider permitting unbelievers to demonstrate their support by participating in the preparation phase. They may also consider permitting the couple to stand together during the dedication, but they should ask the unbelieving spouse to refrain from affirming the promises.

7. **Should parents be required to participate in the preparation session prior to dedicating their children?**

One of the churches I served required parents to attend the preparation session but accommodated parents who were unable to attend by giving them the option to participate remotely or listen/watch a recording of the session. The other church did not require the class, but since the class was presented as part of the dedication process, most parents assumed it was required. I would not encourage parents to participate in a dedication service without there being some assurance that they have considered the promises, understand their implications, and are ready to commit to keeping them.

8. **Is it "Child Dedication" or "Parent Dedication"?**

It probably makes little difference what elders decide to call it, but it is good to be consistent in how you refer to it. My preference has been "Child Dedication" for two reasons. First, even though the dedication of the child involves a commitment from the parents and the church, the pastoral declaration that we use is directed to the child ("Together with your parents who love you dearly and this congregation that cares about the outcome of your faith, I dedicate you to God..."). Second, if we consider this a parent dedication, it seems that parents would only need to dedicate themselves once. Since parents are encouraged to participate in the dedication service every time they welcome a child into their home, it seems fitting that the description of the event should be linked to the child.

More Details

It is surprising how many logistical details need to be worked out and how many special circumstances come up that require attention. The following section contains extra information that we hope you will find helpful as you plan and prepare.

When All Is Said and Done

May the fruit of your dedication services and all your labors abound to all generations. May all the children and families within your ministry be great in God's Kingdom and mighty in the land. Even to the next generation, may these children and their children after them be blessed. May they find their treasure in God through Jesus Christ. May they abound in love, joy, peace, patience, kindness, goodness, faithfulness, gentleness, and self-control. May they never be shaken, and may their names be remembered by the Lord forever!

Child Dedication Resources and Sample Documents

Parental Promises for the Dedication of Children (in Question Format)

1. Do you recognize these children as gifts of God and give heartfelt thanks for God's blessing?

2. Do you now dedicate your children to the Lord who gave them to you, surrendering all worldly claims upon their lives in the hope that they will belong wholly to Jesus Christ forever?

3. Do you pledge, with God's fatherly help, to bring up these children in the discipline and instruction of the Lord, making every effort, with faithfulness, patience, and love, to build the Word of God, the character of Christ, and the joy of the Lord into their lives?

4. Do you promise to provide, through God's blessing, for the physical, emotional, intellectual, and spiritual needs of your children, looking to your own heavenly Father for the wisdom, love, and strength to serve and not use them?

5. Do you promise, God helping you, to make it your regular prayer that, by God's grace, your children will come to trust in Jesus Christ alone for the forgiveness of their sins and for the fulfillment of all His promises to them, even eternal life, and in this faith follow Jesus as Lord and obey His teachings?

Pastoral Pronouncement

Together with your parents who love you dearly and this congregation that cares about the outcome of your faith, I dedicate you to God, surrendering together with them all worldly claims upon your life in the hope that you will belong wholly to Jesus Christ forever.

Parental Promises and the Dedication of Children (with Explanation)

Four times a year, we witness parents standing before the congregation with the children they are dedicating to the Lord. The heart of the child dedication is the five promises. It is important for us all to know that these are promises that parents and the congregation as a whole are making. Notice the words that we speak over every child:

> *Together with your parents who love you dearly **and this congregation** that cares about the outcome of your faith, I dedicate you to God, surrendering together with them all worldly claims upon your life in the hope that you will belong wholly to Jesus Christ forever.*

These words emphasize that parents have two *partners* supporting them as they raise their children in the faith. The first is God, who is committed to declaring His glory from one generation to the next and fulfilling His unstoppable purposes to raise up worshipers in every generation. If God is for these parents and their children, they have all they need. The second partner is "this congregation," the people of this local church committing their support, encouragement, and prayers for these parents in the hope that their children "will belong wholly to Jesus Christ forever."

Since we share responsibility for the faith of *our* children at our local church, it is important that we understand the promises and their implications.

1. **We recognize these children as gifts of God and give heartfelt thanks for God's blessing.**

    Children are a gift—regardless of the timing and circumstances of their arrival. They are not an accident. They are a gift—no matter how they come. They are a gift even when they are not what we expect. They are a gift even when they come with infantile seizures, chromosome irregularities, heart problems, deformities, blindness, tumors, brain damage, respiratory issues, etc. They are a gift when they are vomiting in the middle of the night and displaying their tempers in the grocery store. It is an honor to be entrusted by God with these gifts.

2. **We dedicate our children to the Lord who gave them to us, surrendering all worldly claims upon their lives in the hope that they will belong wholly to Jesus Christ forever.**

   Even though children are a gift of God, He retains *ownership* and sovereign rights over our children. Specifically, He has the right to give and to take on His timetable. He has the right to bring our children to faith in His way, on His schedule, and according to His purpose. And He has the right to lead our children wherever He pleases. Our submission to God's will and purposes for our children is in the context of the hope that our children will belong wholly to Jesus Christ forever.

3. **We pledge as parents that, with God's fatherly help, we will bring up our children in the discipline and instruction of the Lord, making every effort, with faithfulness, patience, and love, to build the Word of God, the character of Christ and the joy of the Lord into their lives.**

   We are committed to faithfully carrying out our Deuteronomy 6:7 and Ephesians 6:4 responsibilities for our children while acknowledging our limitations and ultimate dependence on God for the grace to fulfill them.

4. **We promise to provide, through God's blessing, for the physical, emotional, intellectual, and spiritual needs of our children, looking to our own heavenly Father for the wisdom, love, and strength to serve them and not use them.**

   Here we promise to provide for our children in every way—a promise that would be impossible to keep without the qualifiers "through God's blessing" and "looking to our own heavenly Father." We also are committing to Christ-like, servant-hearted parenting that recognizes children exist for God and for His glory, and not for our personal satisfaction and pleasure.

5. **We promise, God helping us, to make it our regular prayer that, by God's grace, our children will come to trust in Jesus Christ alone for the forgiveness of their sins and for the fulfillment of all His promises to them, even eternal life, and in this faith follow Jesus as Lord and obey His teachings.**

Our greatest desire (and hope) is that God will save our children and that they will passionately follow Jesus. Since, ultimately, we have no control over the hearts of our children, we resolve to earnestly pray to the One who does.

As God raises up one generation after another at our church, we know the joy of the Apostle John who said, "I have no greater joy than to hear that my children are walking in the truth" (3 John 1:4).

Recommended Books

(Titles marked with an asterisk were given to parents attending the Parenting Foundations class at College Park Church in Indianapolis, Indiana.)

- *A Father's Guide to Blessing His Children* by David Michael (Truth78, 2018)
- *Big, Bold, Biblical Prayers for the Next Generation* by David Michael (Truth78, 2018)
- Gospel-Powered Parenting: How the Gospel Shapes and Transforms Parenting by William P. Farley (Phillipsburg, N.J.: P&R Publishing Company, 2009)
- Hints on Child Training by H. Clay Trumbull (Eugene, Ore.: Great Expectations Book Co., 1993). (Note: This book was originally published in 1890)
- Instructing a Child's Heart by Tedd and Margy Tripp (Wapwallopen, Penn.: Shepherd Press, 2008)
- *Mighty Men: The Starter's Guide to Leading Your Family* by John Crotts (Sand Springs, Okla.: Grace and Truth Books, 2004)
- *Mothers: Disciplers of the Next Generations* by Sally Michael (Truth78, 2013)
- *Praying for the Next Generation* by Sally Michael (Truth78, 2022)
- Shepherding a Child's Heart by Tedd Tripp (Wapwallopen, Penn.: Shepherd Press, 1995)
- Teach Them Diligently: How to Use the Scriptures in Child Training by Lou Priolo (Woodruff, S.C.: Timeless Texts, 2000)
- *The Disciple-Making Parent: A Comprehensive Guidebook for Raising Your Children to Love and Follow Jesus Christ* by Chap Bettis (Vestavia, Ala.: Diamond Hill Publishing, 2016)
- *Zealous, 7 Commitments for the Discipleship of the Next Generations* by David Michael (Truth78, 2021)

Pastor Instructions for Dedication Service

Every dedication service will need to fit the traditions, culture, and style of the individual church. Below are detailed instructions for conducting a quarterly dedication service in one particular church, which may be helpful and provide some guidance and ideas for planning a dedication in another church.

In the two churches I served, there were two pastors involved in the dedication, which we identified as the presiding pastor and the assisting pastor. As Pastor for the Next Generation, I always favored the assisting pastor role and would invite different pastoral colleagues to serve as the presiding pastor. I was eager for the church to see all the pastors giving leadership and to hear them express their hearts and vision for the next generation.

I also wanted my colleagues to experience the pastoral privilege and joy of dedicating a child, and the special pastoral connection with the dedicating parents and child.

Instructions for Presiding Pastor

Prepare Opening Words for the Dedication Service

This brief word (1-2 minutes) directed to the parents and the congregation can be a word of vision or a challenge that sets a biblical and God-centered tone for the service—a tone that suggests *important, weighty,* and *solemn*. It is nice if you can link it to something like a song the congregation has just sung, a prominent news event, the current sermon series, a Fighter Verse, something from the *front burner* of personal meditations, or something from your area of ministry.

Memorize the Words of Dedication

…together with your parents who love you dearly and this congregation that cares about the outcome of your faith, I dedicate you to God, surrendering together with them all worldly claims upon your life in the hope that you will belong wholly to Jesus Christ forever.

On the Day of the Dedication Service

1. Please wear... [provide guidelines for appropriate clothing for the service].
2. Make sure you have the cue sheet with the names of each dedicating parent and their child/ren.
3. Report to the [meeting location] by [meeting time] to be fitted with a microphone and participate in the service rehearsal.
4. Twenty minutes before the service, meet with the assisting pastor and the parents [at your prearranged meeting place]. Be sure to personally connect with the parents of the children you will be dedicating and confirm the accuracy and pronunciation of the names of the parents and their children.
5. Once all the parents have arrived, welcome them and offer the follow information and instruction:

Pre-Service Session with Dedication Families

- **Introduce**—Assisting Pastor, Service Coordinator, Dedication Coordinator, etc.
- **Confirm** that parents received a dedication packet when they arrived (including the baton, if you're using a baton).
- **Service Flow**—Walk through the elements of the service leading up to the dedication. Identify the point when the families should step out of the service (usually at the beginning of the last song before the dedication) and meet back at the gathering spot.
- **Parents return to the sanctuary at the designated time** in the service and bring the baton with them [if you're using a baton]—although, if they think the baton will be a distraction for the child, they can feel free to leave it behind.
- **Line up** in alphabetical order (unless directed otherwise).
- **Preferably fathers hold the child,** but it is okay if the child needs his mom to hold him. Moms could place a hand on the child during dedication if they would like to.

- **Identify the center couple** (or couples) and explain they should stop at the center point on the stage. Other couples space themselves out elbow distance between them.
- **Respond to the promise/questions with "I DO"** (not "we do").
- **Respond heartily,** like they mean it. It will emphasize the point if you have them practice it.
- **After each child is dedicated, the family should step down to main floor level** using the stairs closest to them. The first couple should move to the center, and this time couples should space themselves at arm's length to make room for friends and family to gather around them.
- **After the last child is dedicated, explain that the assisting pastor will step forward, invite friends and family to gather around them and lead in prayer.** Also explain that, at the end, you will lift your hands and pronounce a benediction (blessing) over them. At that time, they are free to return to their seats.
- **Encourage parents to relax;** don't fret if child gets fussy or upset. Don't leave—we will manage and count it as music to the Lord's ears.
- **Ask if there are any questions.**

6. Just before dismissing the parents, invite the assisting pastor to pray.

7. Sit toward the front so that you can quickly step to the stage and begin your opening remarks as the parents are taking their positions on stage behind you. Include in your remarks that the parents are holding a baton symbolizing the passing of faith from one generation to the next.

8. At the conclusion of your remarks, turn and face the parents and ask them the following questions one at a time. After each question, look up at one of the couples and wait for them to respond with a hearty "I do" before moving to the next question.

- **Do you recognize** these children as a gift of God and give heartfelt thanks for God's blessing?

- **Do you now dedicate** your children to the Lord who gave them to you, surrendering all worldly claims upon their lives in the hope that they will belong wholly to Jesus Christ forever?

- **Do you pledge** as parents, with God's fatherly help, to bring up these children in the discipline and instruction of the Lord, making every effort, with faithfulness, patience, and love, to build the Word of God, the character of Christ, and the joy of the Lord into their lives?

- **Do you promise** to provide, through God's blessing, for the physical, emotional, intellectual, and spiritual needs of your children, looking to your own heavenly Father for the wisdom, love, and strength to serve them and not use them?

- **Do you promise,** God helping you, to make it your regular prayer that by God's grace your children will come to trust in Jesus Christ alone for the forgiveness of their sins and for the fulfillment of all His promises to them, even eternal life, and in this faith follow Jesus as Lord and obey His teachings?

9. After the last question, move to the left (stage right) and stand beside the first couple. As you are moving, you may want to address the congregation and say something like,

    After each child is dedicated, we will invite you to join with us in saying "amen." This congregational "amen" is an opportunity for us to express our commitment to stand with these parents and to support their efforts to nurture the faith of these children in whatever way God may lead us.

10. Introduce the first parents (stage right) and the child (using the child's full name)—"This is Ruth and Jerry Michael and their fourth child, David Gerald." Place your right hand on the child's head and pronounce the words of dedication.

- Try to make eye contact with the child as you are dedicating him.
- Avoid a power-struggle with the child over touching his head. If your hand is upsetting him, move it to his back or a limb and speak quickly.
- Try to have these words solidly memorized.

[Child's name], together with your parents who love you dearly and this congregation that cares about the outcome of your faith, I dedicate you to God, surrendering together with them all worldly claims upon your life in the hope that you will belong wholly to Jesus Christ forever. And all the people said amen!

Note: For the sake of time, when parents are dedicating more than one child, dedicate the children together—"Silas, Sarah, and Jonathan, together with your parents who love you dearly..." If there are two children, place a hand on each child. If more than two, move your hands back and forth as you pronounce the words of dedication.

11. After you dedicate the child, step aside and signal the parents to move to floor level in front of the stage while the assisting pastor introduces the next couple on the opposite end. Proceed, alternating until the last child is dedicated.

12. After the last child is dedicated, move to the floor level, and stand with one of the dedicating families while the assisting pastor invites friends and family members to come forward and surround the dedicating families and then leads the congregation in a prayer of dedication and benediction.

Instructions for the Assisting Pastor

Pre-Service Preparation

Prepare a 2-minute dedication prayer in advance of the service that
- exalts the Giver and Sustainer of life.
- reflects our heart and vision for the next generation.
- seeks grace for the parents to keep the promises they made and for church as we labor together with the parents to raise these children in the fear and the joy of the Lord.

The service plan usually considers this a time of "elder prayer," which means you may be given names of missionaries and those facing needs of various kinds within the church. With only two minutes to work with, I usually don't include any of these items unless there is something particularly urgent.

Sample prayers are available in the back of the booklet *Big, Bold, Biblical Prayers* (see Truth78.org).

Earnestly seek the Lord for help not only for the words but the heart to pray the words with passion and emotion that will give rise to heartfelt "amens" from the people.

Parents will receive a hard copy of your prayer, so please email a copy to the [e.g., Children's Ministry Assistant] no later than the Monday before the dedication service.

Memorize the Words of Dedication

> …together with your parents who love you dearly and this congregation that cares about the outcome of your faith, I dedicate you to God, surrendering together with them all worldly claims upon your life in the hope that you will belong wholly to Jesus Christ forever.

On the Day of the Dedication Service

1. Please wear a jacket with dress pants, dress shoes, and an open-collar dress shirt.

2. Report to the sanctuary by 7 a.m. to be fitted with a microphone and participate in the service rehearsal. Check with [children's ministry assistant] ahead of time to make sure there are no last-minute changes.

3. Twenty minutes before the service, meet with the presiding pastor and the parents outside the sanctuary entrance across from the East Room. Be sure to personally connect with the parents of the children you will be dedicating and confirm the accuracy and pronunciation of the names of the parents and their children.

4. Once all the parents have arrived, the presiding pastor will welcome them, offer the following information and instruction, and invite you to pray for the parents as they are dismissed.

5. At the designated point in the service, meet the parents back at the pre-service meeting location where they will line up in alphabetical order (unless otherwise instructed) and prepare to enter the auditorium.

6. Lead the parents onto the stage at the service coordinator's signal, stopping at stage left to allow the parents to walk past you. After the parents are in place, move toward the end couple and face the presiding pastor.

7. After the parents respond to the last promise/question, the presiding pastor will move to the left (stage right) and stand beside the first couple. He will introduce the parents and dedicate the child.

8. Then you will introduce the parents and child at the opposite end (stage left). Use each child's full name in the introductions—"This is Ruth and Jerry Michael and their fourth child, David Gerald." Place your right hand on the back of the child's head, shoulders (or wherever he lets you), and pronounce the words of dedication.
    - Try to make eye contact with the child as you are dedicating them
    - Avoid a power-struggle with the child over touching his head. If your hand is upsetting him, move it to his back or a limb and speak quickly.
    - Try to have these words solidly memorized.

    [Child's name], together with your parents who love you dearly and this congregation that cares about the outcome of your faith, I dedicate you to God, surrendering together with them all worldly claims upon your life in the hope that you will belong wholly to Jesus Christ forever. And all the people said amen!

    Note: For the sake of time, when parents are dedicating more than one child, dedicate the children together— "Silas, Sarah, and Jonathan, together with your parents who love you dearly..." If there are two children, place a hand on each child. If more than two, move your hands back and forth as you pronounce the words of dedication.

9. After you dedicate the child, step aside and signal the parents to move to floor level in front of the stage while the presiding pastor

introduces the next couple on the opposite end. Proceed, alternating until the last child is dedicated.

10. When the last child is dedicated, invite friends and family to come forward and surround the couples. Give them 30-60 seconds to assemble, but you will likely need to start praying before everyone gets there.

11. As you close the dedication prayer, don't say "amen"—just transition to the blessing/benediction by lifting your hands. It is helpful to have this memorized, so you can lift both hands and try to look toward each child as you pronounce the following benediction:

> *And now children,*
> *May you dwell in the shelter of the Most High*
> *and rest in the shadow of the Almighty.*
> *May the Lord be your refuge*
> *and the God in whom you trust.*
> *May His faithfulness be your shield and rampart.*
> *May the Lord command His angels concerning you*
> *to guard you in all your ways.*
> *May He answer you when you call*
> *and be with you in trouble.*
> *May the Lord deliver you and honor you.*
> *May He satisfy you with long life*
> *and show you His salvation.*
> *Amen.*

Sample Prayer of Dedication

(More examples of dedication prayers can be found the booklet *Big, Bold, Biblical Prayers for the Next Generation* (see Truth78.org).

Heavenly Father, we come before You and worship You as our covenant-keeping God. Not one promise of Yours has failed. You speak, and it is done. You command, and it comes to pass. So Lord, we look to You as the source of all that these parents need in order to keep the promises they have just made.

We pray that each of these children will one day stand in Christ—fully absolved of their sins. We ask that You give them such confidence in You that they trust You completely without a hint of unbelief as they walk on the path that You have set before them.

Teach them to delight in Your Word. Teach them to have no will but Yours. Give them the certainty that everything You do is not only good but the very best that it can be. Teach them to leave every concern in Your almighty hands.

If Satan should demand to sift them like wheat, I pray that their faith will not fail. Do not let the devil undermine their trust in You. Instead, may all their earthly troubles produce steadfastness. And let steadfastness have its full effect, that they may one day be perfect and complete.

And, Lord, we thank You for the parents that You have given to these children and for the faith You have given them to make these promises. O, Lord, may their faith increase as they go forward in the strength, and the power, and the wisdom that You provide.

O, God, may this next generation surpass us all in faith and in fruitfulness for the sake of Your name and the spread of the gospel. Make them bold and courageous proclaimers of truth in this nation and in all nations, to this people and to all the peoples of the earth—until You come, our Glorious King, and all Your ransomed home to bring—when we anew Your song will sing "Hallelujah! What a Savior!" in whose name we pray.

> *And now children,*
> *May you dwell in the shelter of the Most High*
> *and rest in the shadow of the Almighty.*

*May the Lord be your refuge
and the God in whom you trust.
May His faithfulness be your shield and rampart.
May the Lord command His angels concerning you
to guard you in all your ways.
May He answer you when you call
and be with you in trouble.
May the Lord deliver you and honor you.
May He satisfy you with long life
and show you His salvation.
Amen.*

Sample Pastor Letter (to go inside the baton)

Dear Katie,

This letter is part of a College Park Church tradition that goes back to a time long before you were born. On the third Sunday in May 2019, your mom and dad were given the baton that I assume you have just opened. Our hope is that they have presented this to you on your 18th birthday so that you might know what we were thinking and praying at the time of your dedication.

In addition to this letter, there should be four other items in your baton:

- A copy of the promises that your mom and dad publicly affirmed before the congregation and the words of dedication that were pronounced over you. I pray that, by the time you are 18 years old, you will be able to testify to the benefit of having parents who took these promises seriously. I first met your mom and dad around the time your big sister was born and have had the privilege of getting to know them and serving with them at College Park. They have been among our most faithful workers serving our preschool children at the eight o'clock hour. I have been amazed and grateful for their commitment and impact they are having on these young lives. I hope you have realized, by the time you read this letter, the blessing you have received through the parents God has given you. If God is pleased to give you children someday, I am praying that you will be as faithful to God and to your children as your parents have been.

- The prayer of dedication will help you understand the desires of our hearts for you as your parents dedicated you to the Lord. Please notice first that our earnest prayer was that you will one day stand blameless in the presence Christ. We had in mind Psalm 1:5, which teaches that, apart from Christ, you cannot stand in the day of judgment. Our desire is that you WILL stand, which means my greatest desire is that you are *in Christ* as you read this letter on your 18th birthday. Also notice the end of the prayer that our desire is for God to use you to reach the nations. Just before you were dedicated, our Pastor for Global Outreach helped the congregation see the connection between the dedication of our children and God's purposes to reach the nations. Whether or not you anticipate investing your life as a missionary, our prayer is that you will be a bold and courageous proclaimer of truth.
- You will also find the dedication certificate, which is meant to commemorate this significant moment in your life. You can see that the text we used for the certificate is taken from the end of Psalm 91 and is also the benediction that was pronounced over you at the end of the dedication prayer.
- Finally, we have included a list with the names of the other children who were dedicated on this day. I wonder if you know any of them.

As you enter this next exciting season of life, may our Lord Jesus Christ strengthen you, hold you, and sustain you and your hope in Him to your very last breath. May you always feel the hands of God's love holding you fast and the chords of His eternal purpose drawing you closer to Christ.

For God's glory and for your everlasting joy,

David Michael, Pastor for the Next Generations

PART 2: PREPARING YOUNG PEOPLE FOR BAPTISM

Young Baptism Approach and Process

Introduction

In this guide, I am proposing an approach that brings church and home together for the preparation of a young person for baptism. In the introduction to *Established in the Faith*, a companion booklet to this guide, I wrote how this approach to baptism preparation grew out of my desire to be faithful to my calling as a father and shepherd in my home. Most church leaders affirm that parents have primary responsibility for the discipleship of their children, but we can sometimes unwittingly communicate that the parents' job is to get their kids to church and let the *professionals* take it from there. Church leadership is responsible to oversee the ordinance of baptism, but it is important that we fulfill that responsibility without overlooking the significant responsibility, privilege, and blessing that belongs to parents. This is the main reason I am promoting this approach, but there are other practical reasons as well.

I am persuaded that, when parents are involved, the young person (hereafter referred to as "student") is often better prepared. The parent knows the student better. They are more likely to see evidence of grace and spiritual growth, which can be affirmed in the preparation process. Parents are also more likely to observe patterns of sin and unbelief, which also can be addressed.

Since one of the priorities in baptism preparation is to discern if the student is born again, it makes sense that we would involve the people in that preparation who have observed the student the most. In Matthew 7:13-23, Jesus makes clear that the way we discern the difference between a person who is truly on the narrow path that leads to life and the person who is on the broad path that leads to destruction is by the fruit of that person's life. Healthy trees (true children of God in Christ) bear good fruit. Diseased trees (those dead in their sins) bear bad fruit. We cannot depend upon good behavior (verse 15) or upon the words they may say or do (verse 22). A parent has more opportunity to observe the fruit in the student's life than the church leader, who may only see the student once or twice a week.

Another practical benefit of this approach is that when, for whatever reason, the student is not ready to be baptized, it is best when parents come to that conclusion first. If it's just the church leader who has the concern after working with the student, he has to explain, and sometimes defend, his reasons to the parents, risking potential hurt or conflict.

The last benefit I'll mention is that this approach takes pressure off students to proceed with baptism if they or their parents feel they are not yet ready. A common approach to preparation that churches have taken is to invite students to attend a baptism class. These classes vary in length, after which there is an opportunity to be baptized. With this model, it can seem to the student that baptism is the goal of the class and thus marks successful completion of the class. If a student goes through the class and chooses not to be baptized, or if the leader does not believe the student is ready, it can seem like a failure, and that can be embarrassing among the student's peers.

This guide presents an approach that takes into account these concerns, values, and convictions. The preparation process explained here was developed and implemented in the two churches I served. It is not the only way to do it, and there are logistics that can certainly be improved. My hope is that presenting this model will serve other ministry leaders who can adapt it for use in their churches.

Securing Support from Church Leadership

When introducing a new or revised baptism preparation process, it is wise (and in some cases required) to seek support from the elders/senior leadership of the church. There are at least three reasons why this is important.

1. This honors church leadership and affirms the responsibility they have for overseeing the ordinance of baptism.
2. It is important for leadership to have the opportunity to review and approve the instructional materials and recommended resources that are used in the preparation process.

3. In this suggested process, there are requirements and expectations of the candidate, parents, and church leadership that should be affirmed. It is helpful for those participating in the process to understand that the standards are backed by the church leadership.

I found it helpful to prepare a proposal to the elders detailing the suggested process with rationale for why there is value to implement a separate youth baptism process. (See the Youth Baptism Resources and Sample Documents section for a sample proposal.)

Steps in the Process

1. **Invitation to Consider Baptism**

    Once a year, an invitation is sent to parents of perspective baptism candidates. In the churches I served, baptism candidates included young people between the ages of 11 and 18 years who had not been baptized, and younger children whose parents had asked to be contacted. Included with this communication is information that explains the preparation process and an application parents are asked to complete. (Again, see the Youth Baptism Resources and Sample Document section toward the end of this booklet for the overview for parents and church leaders.)

    A different communication is sent to parents who began the process at an earlier time but decided at that point that their student was not ready to move ahead. This letter simply reminds them that we are beginning the cycle again and invites them to check in with their student to see if they are ready to continue the process.

2. **Parent/Mentor Orientation Session**

    Parents who indicate a desire to begin the process are invited to the Parent/Mentor Orientation Session. It is helpful if both parents attend, but be sure to emphasize that the student should *not* attend this meeting. Parents and mentors often assume that the students should accompany them, and it is awkward for everyone if they show up.

    This session usually requires about two hours and is designed to pursue the following goals:
    - Establish rapport with each parent/mentor.

- Foster a sense of camaraderie among the parents/mentors.
- Motivate the parents/mentors to responsibly guide and support their students through the preparation process.
- Sufficiently prepare the parents/mentors for the task.
- Corporately seek God's help.

A typical session format looks like this:

Setting a God-Centered Tone—Welcome the parents/mentors, present the agenda for the meeting, and introduce a text that can set an appropriate tone for the session. For example, John 6:29 says, "This is the work of God, that you believe in him whom he has sent." Take five minutes to emphasize that believing in Jesus is the work of God and not man. Explain that, as parents/mentors, we are putting ourselves in a place where we can see evidence of God's work in a student's life and encourage growth. Conclude this with a brief prayer.

Introductions—Invite the parents/mentors to introduce themselves and ask them to describe the student they represent. Consider asking them to talk about the spiritual development they have observed in the student and what precipitated their desire to move ahead with baptism preparation. If there is time, it is helpful to facilitate conversation about their expectations for this preparation process. Conclude the time by inviting the parents/mentors to take a few minutes to pray for each other and the students.

Review the *Established in the Faith* Booklet—Even though parent/mentors can read the booklet for themselves, taking the time to go through it point by point ensures that they have read it and provides the opportunity to emphasize and clarify important components of the process. Usually, this review prompts questions and discussion.

Review Remaining Steps and Important Dates in the Process—Before concluding this meeting, communicate the date for the combined meeting with parents/mentors and students as well as the date for the baptism service. Plan a minimum of eight weeks between the parents/mentors' meeting and the combined meeting. Allow three to four weeks between the combined meeting and the baptism service. Parents/mentors should aim to complete their individual sessions before the combined session. Distribute copies of the parent/mentor and student response forms, which will be submitted following the combined meeting. (See samples of these forms at Truth78.org/dedication-baptism-resources)

3. **Parent/Mentor Individual Sessions with Students**

   Encourage parents/mentors to have at least six separate, one-on-one sessions with the students. The *Established in the Faith* booklet gives suggestions for how to structure these sessions. Three or four weeks into this period, it is helpful to send a note or call the parents/mentors to see how they are doing and remind them of upcoming dates.

4. **Parent/Mentor and Student Group Session**

   During this session, parents/mentors and students come together for a half-day meeting with one or two church leaders. Students will share their testimonies with the group and review the meaning of baptism. They will also be introduced to the church's history and distinctives, the meaning of membership, and a review of other important membership documents (such as the church covenant and affirmation of faith). At the end of this meeting, students and parents/mentors submit their response forms.

5. **Interview with Baptism/Membership Team**

   After the parent/mentor and the student have indicated the student's readiness to move ahead with baptism (and, in some cases, church membership), the student will be interviewed. My practice was to identify an interview team that included an elder, an adult leader who has regular contact with the student (e.g., a Sunday school teacher or a small group leader) and an older youth who has already been baptized. During this interview, the student gives his testimony and responds to informal questions concerning faith and church membership. (For helpful resources for this team, see the Youth Baptism Resources and Sample Documents section in this booklet and Truth78.org/dedication-baptism-resources)

6. **Baptism Service**

   If the baptism/membership team recommends the student, he will be scheduled for baptism in an upcoming service. The service will vary depending on the traditions and practices of the church. In one church, we offered a special midweek youth baptism service annually. The service usually included worship led by an all-youth worship team, student testimonies, a pastoral message to the students, the baptisms, and a prayer for the students.

   We involved the parents in two ways. When giving their testimonies, the students stood in the front of the church with their parents standing behind them. As each student began his testimony, he introduced his parents and then, during the testimony, the students were encouraged to acknowledge their parents' influence in their lives when appropriate.

   When the testimonies were complete, the students made their way to one end of the baptismal and parents stood on the opposite end. After each baptism, parents helped their student out of the water and wrapped him with a white robe or large towel. After the last student was baptized, family and friends gathered around each student and prayed for him.

Pastoral Considerations

Age for Baptism

Sooner or later, leaders in churches that practice believer's baptism need to decide if there should be a minimum age set for a child to be baptized. There are various positions on this. Some churches set no minimum age and will baptize a child if he can make a credible profession of faith. There are also churches that prefer not to baptize children at all and require a minimum age of 18.

Although there is not specific biblical guidance addressing age, I have recommended that children not be baptized before 11 years. Admittedly, this is somewhat arbitrary and is a matter of pastoral judgment. The recommendation also fits with a broader discipleship strategy that I promoted for the children growing up in the churches I served, which is why it worked well to specify that age.

This is not to suggest that every 11-year-old who professes faith in Christ should be baptized. Many should not. But, in my experience, before age 11 there is a greater likelihood of a child not being ready. It is hard to start the preparation process with a child, determine he is not ready, and then ask him to wait. Having a target age in mind gives parents the ability to explain to their child that he can begin exploring baptism when he is 11 (or another age), making it an exciting milestone to which he can look forward.

This can be a very emotional topic for some parents, and thus pastoral sensitivity is needed. It is certainly reasonable for a parent to ask, "If my eight-year-old expresses a desire to be baptized, why should I refuse?" Most of the time, the parents I worked with were satisfied with the reasons I outlined in an article entitled, "Concerning the Age of Baptism for Children: Reasons for Waiting." This article is included in the appendix of the *Established in the Faith* booklet.

I also recommended to parents that they read Art Murphy's *The Faith of a Child: A Step-by-Step Guide to Salvation for Your Child* and Dennis Gunderson's *Your Child's Profession of Faith,* both of which are excellent resources to help parents consider this question.

When You Think a Student Is Too Young

One of the benefits of this approach to baptism preparation is that it avoids (though does not eliminate) the potential disagreement between pastors/elders and parents on whether their children are ready for baptism or not. If the child is not ready, this process puts the parents in the place where they can be the first to discern this. The baptism/membership team is the final sieve where the parental assessment is confirmed or not. Although there are occasions when the elder must overrule the parental assessment, such occasions will be rare if the parent/mentor is well-prepared and takes his responsibility seriously.

The Father/Mentor

This process is primarily designed to help leaders faithfully and effectively prepare young people for baptism. Secondarily, it provides an opportunity to support and equip fathers in their shepherding role.

Most of the husbands/fathers I interact with understand that they are the spiritual leaders in their homes. However, not all of them have a clear picture of what that leadership looks like. From my informal surveys over the years, I assumed that more than half of the men in an average church grew up with absent or unbelieving fathers. Of those who had believing fathers, usually less than 15 percent would say that their father was a good example of spiritual leadership in the home. Only a small fraction of the men would say that their fathers had a clear enough vision for manhood and leadership in the home to be intentional about training their sons to be spiritual, shepherd-like, servant-leaders in the home. I have not yet met a husband/father who had no desire to be a faithful shepherd in his home, but I have encountered many who never had the opportunity to learn how. May God grant the grace to us as leaders in the church to better serve, support, and equip the next generation of husbands and fathers.

Considering this need in the church, this process is designed to affirm the father's shepherding role in his home. It invites him especially into the preparation process and offers him an opportunity to exercise his God-given spiritual privilege and responsibility. One of the most gratifying aspects of this experience is seeing fathers happily accept this opportunity and witnessing the positive impact it has on the man and his son or daughter. In almost every case, the wives have not felt left out of the process but rather rejoice seeing their husbands giving spiritual direction to their son or daughter.

To be clear, this approach does not depend on the father serving in the parent/mentor role. It is not always the best fit for him to do it. At times, it makes more sense for mom, or both mom and dad, or a grandparent or another person who is investing in the discipleship of the student to take this role.

Parent/Mentor

If the father is present in the home and is a professing believer, encourage him to assume the role of parent/mentor. In some cases, parents have expressed a desire to be *co-mentors*, which is perfectly fine; but, as much as possible, still emphasize the father's unique role and responsibility. If the father is clearly not a believer, is absent from the home, or is unwilling to be involved, encourage the mother, grandparent, or another mature believer to assume the mentor role. Single mothers of sons often see this as an opportunity to connect their son with a godly father figure. This can help to establish an ongoing discipleship relationship that will benefit the son and support the mother in her parenting role.

You will likely run into situations where the father is a professing believer but there are doubts about his ability to do the job. He may be spiritually weak and immature. He may be struggling with his faith or have some unresolved sin in his life. Such men may feel threatened by this process. Do not let these concerns hinder encouraging a man to assume responsibility for the spiritual care of his children. Usually, this process confronts such a man with his need. It may motivate him to either take some positive steps toward growth or simply not follow through with the process. A man who does not follow through with the process provides us with an opportunity to check in with him and inquire. If the man is unable to guide his child through this process with integrity, consider suspending the preparation process and working with the father until he is ready. This helps the father see the impact that his spiritual condition has on his children, and it may be what God uses to help him grow and mature in his responsibility.

When a Parent/Mentor or Student Decides to Wait

In the first meeting with the parents/mentors, it is helpful to communicate that they might begin the process and soon realize that the student is not ready. Assure them that this is common and it is better to wait than to encourage a student to move forward when he is not ready. Usually, around 25 percent and sometimes as many as 50 percent of those who begin the process do not complete the cycle. In most cases, the parent/mentor recognizes that the student lacks sufficient understanding or spiritual maturity and wants to give the student more time to learn and grow in faith. Waiting can actually be an important part of the discipleship process and be a God-ordained opportunity. Guard against expressing any negative connotation with pausing the baptism preparation process.

Be sure to alert parent/mentors to the critical moment in Step 4 of the individual session[11] when they invite the student to decisively affirm his faith. Some students have said "no" at this point, which can be upsetting to parents. When this happens, it is important to help the parents discern what the spiritual issues are, suggest ways for them to respond, and offer assurance and hope.

---

11 See Step 4 in the *Established in the Faith* booklet.

Should fathers or other special people baptize a student?

Affirming the father's spiritual role in this process may raise the question of the father baptizing his son or daughter. Even though the Bible does not give specific guidance on the question, I recommend church leadership give this matter careful consideration. Opening the door to this practice might elevate the role of fathering too much or diminish the uniqueness of the ordinance and responsibility of the church leaders. The tradition of an authorized pastor/elder of the church performing the baptism goes back hundreds of years and seems to be rooted in something crucial that could be quickly lost and not easily recovered. In the end, we agreed to err on the side of preserving the history and tradition of a pastor/elder being the main person performing the baptisms.

Keep in mind the risk of putting too much unintended emphasis on the baptizer over the baptism itself. If the expectation is that fathers baptize, it can be tricky if the father is divorced and not living in the home or if he is not a believer. Also, opening the door for families to request a particular pastor, family member, friend, or Sunday school teacher can create another set of less-than-important issues to manage. My solution to this problem was to maintain the standard of an authorized pastor/elder presiding over the baptism while allowing a dad or other special person to assist with the baptism. Typically, the presiding pastor and the assistant stand in the water on either side of the student. The presiding pastor asks the baptism questions, makes the pronouncement, and then together with the assistant immerses the student and brings him up out of the water.

Youth Baptism Resources and Sample Documents

Sample Proposal for a Revised Baptism Preparation Process

Proposal

1. That the elders establish the proposed process for preparing young people (under age 18) for baptism at our church as outlined in the "Preparing Young People for Baptism and Church Membership: An Overview for Parents and Church Leaders" document following this proposal.

2. To ask every candidate for baptism to respond publicly to the following questions:

    > *Are you now trusting in Jesus Christ alone for the forgiveness of your sins and for the fulfillment of all His promises to you, even eternal life?*
    >
    > *Do you renounce Satan in all his works and all his ways?*
    >
    > *Do you intend, with God's help, to obey Jesus' teachings and to follow Him as your Lord and obey His teachings?*

    and to publicly baptize candidates in the name of the Father, Son, and Holy Spirit with wording similar to this:

    > *On your profession of faith in Jesus Christ and in obedience to His command, I now baptize you in the name of the Father, the Son, and the Holy Spirit.*

3. That children be encouraged (or required) to wait until at least age 11 before being baptized.
    - This is a recommendation, not a requirement.
    - There is no biblical instruction concerning a minimum age for baptism.

- The age recommendation is a matter of pastoral judgment.
- This recommendation fits with our broader discipleship strategy for children growing up in Christian homes.
- Children above age 10 are more likely
  - to think independently.
  - to remember the baptism experience.
  - to appreciate the importance and significance of baptism.
  - to have the spiritual maturity and intellectual capacity for a deeper understanding of and appreciation for the gospel.

4. That children be encouraged to wait until after baptism to participate in the Lord's Supper.
   - This is a recommendation and not a requirement.
   - There is no biblical instruction concerning a minimum age for taking the Lord's Supper.
   - It should be considered that the historic position within many branches of the Church is that baptism must precede the partaking of the Lord's Supper.
   - Many of the reasons for encouraging children to wait for baptism apply to the Lord's Supper.
   - It seems reasonable and fitting to welcome a young person to the Lord's table after (rather than before) he has publicly confessed faith in Christ and followed Him in the obedience of baptism. (See the "Children and the Lord's Supper" article in this booklet for an example of how this could be communicated to parents.)

5. That our church establishes a process for preparing young people (under age 18) for baptism that includes the following components:
   - Mentor Orientation Meeting (60-90 minutes)
   - Six One-on-One Mentor Sessions with Candidate (6-plus hours)
     - Preparing the Student

- Understanding the Gospel
- Assurance of Salvation
- Affirmation of Faith
- The Meaning of Baptism
- Preparing a Testimony
  - Candidate Testimony
  - Preparation for Church Membership Seminar (3 hours)
  - Candidate Interview with an Elder (30-45 minutes)
  - Baptism Service

Handouts accompanying this proposal include

- "Preparing Young People for Baptism & Church Membership: An Overview for Parents and Church Leaders." (This article follows.)
- "Concerning the Age of Baptism for Children: Reasons for Waiting" (See the appendix of the *Established in the Faith* booklet.)
- "Children and the Lord's Supper" (This article follows.)

Preparing Young People for Baptism and Church Membership: An Overview for Parents and Church Leaders

Introduction

Faithfully preparing a young person to follow the Lord in the obedience of baptism is an important responsibility entrusted to Christian parents and to the church. Our elders affirm that parents are responsible for instructing their children in the Christian faith and overseeing their spiritual development. We also affirm that the church is responsible for facilitating and overseeing the discipleship ministry of the church and for sustaining and guarding the ordinance of baptism. Therefore, it is fitting for leaders of the church and parents to work together in preparing young people for baptism.

Primary Goals of this process
- Glorify Christ and His redeeming work.
- Discern the authenticity of the candidate's faith and readiness for baptism.
- Lead the candidate to a solid understanding of the gospel and the meaning of baptism.
- Prepare the candidate to give a publicly credible profession of faith.

Secondary Goals of this process
- Encourage, support, and equip the spiritual leader of the home for the discipleship of his/her children.
- Provide an opportunity for the candidate to publicly affirm his intention and desire to follow Jesus in a decisive and memorable way.
- Prepare and equip the candidate for membership in the local church.
- Provide an opportunity for the immediate family and the wider community of believers to publicly affirm, support, encourage, and pray for the candidate.

Youth Baptism Preparation Cycle

A Letter of Invitation is sent at the beginning of the cycle to parents of prospective baptism candidates. Prospective candidates include young people between the ages of 11 and 18 who have not been baptized and younger children whose parents have asked to be contacted. This letter explains the preparation process, communicates important dates, and provides a link to an online response form.

Parental Consent before beginning the preparation process is expected for candidates under age 18.

Identifying a Parent/Mentor
- Each candidate will need a mentor to lead him through the first phase of this process.

- Candidates in the same family may share one parent/mentor, but the parent/mentor will be encouraged to meet with each candidate separately.
- The candidate's father is encouraged to be the mentor if he is a believer and living in the home.
- If the father is not a believer and/or not living in the home, the candidate's mother, grandparent, or another mature believer should assume this responsibility.
- If neither parent is a believer, the candidate may select (or seek help in finding) a mentor who can lead the candidate through the preparation process and who is willing to assist and encourage the young person in his walk with the Lord following the baptism.

The Parent/Mentor Orientation and Training Session (60-90 minutes) is designed to help prepare mentors for their significant role in the preparation process. This session is for the parent/mentors only. Candidates do not attend this session. This session will provide an opportunity for mentors to get acquainted with each other and be equipped to prepare their candidate for baptism.

Individual One-on-One Sessions Between Mentor and Candidate (recommend weekly sessions for six weeks)

Candidate is led by his/her parent/mentor through each the following steps.

1. Preparing the Student
2. Understanding the Gospel
3. Assurance of Salvation
4. Affirmation of Faith
5. The Meaning of Baptism
6. Preparing a Testimony

Each cycle provides eight weeks for the mentors to complete the sessions with the candidate. Usually, mentors will cover one step per session. It can take more or less time depending on the candidate's maturity and prior understanding. If a mentor decides that more time is needed with the candidate, he can take the next step in the process in a subsequent cycle.

Testimony

We encourage candidates to give their testimony at least one time prior to their interview and baptism. Perhaps the youth staff could arrange a time for them to give their testimony in a small group or during one of our youth gatherings. Also, parents can arrange a time for them to share their testimony when friends or family are gathered.

Pre-Membership Session

Whether or not the candidate plans to pursue formal church membership, we encourage all candidates to attend this pre-membership session (2-3 hours). The aim of this class is to help young people understand the significance of the church and the meaning of membership. They will review our church covenant, explore our historical roots, and be introduced to our values and affirmation of faith.

Baptism/Membership Interview

Once the parent/mentor communicates that the candidate is ready to move forward with baptism (and, in some cases, church membership) the candidate will be interviewed. The goal of this interview is to hear the candidate's profession of faith and confirm that there is a sufficient understanding of the gospel and the meaning of baptism. The interview team will include at least one church leader and another adult who may have a significant role in the young person's life (perhaps a youth worker, Sunday school teacher, or small group leader). If the candidate desires to proceed with church membership, the interviewers will explore the candidate's understanding of the church covenant and membership.

Baptism Service

If the baptism/membership team recommends the candidate for baptism, the candidate will be scheduled for an upcoming baptism service. An approved candidate may participate in a regular baptism service. Or perhaps the church could explore the possibility of planning an annual youth baptism service that includes worship, candidate testimonies, a pastoral charge to the candidates, the baptism, and time for family and friends to pray for the candidates.

Children and the Lord's Supper

Sooner or later, a child who is regularly sitting through a Sunday morning worship service is bound to ask something like, "Why can't I have a *snack* like everyone else?" So, it is not surprising that one of the most frequent questions I am asked in children's ministry is, "When should my child take the Lord's Supper?" What follows is my attempt to answer that question.

A General Response

When people inquire about children taking the Lord's Supper, I have two perspectives to share with them. The first is that our communion services are open to all present, including children, who are

1. trusting in Jesus Christ alone for the forgiveness of their sins and the fulfillment of all His promises to us (including eternal life) and
2. who intend to follow Him as Lord and obey His commandments.

Therefore, children are welcome to participate in the Lord's Supper:
- when they can understand its significance,
- when they are able to give a credible profession of faith in Christ,
- and when they can express their desire and intention to follow the Lord in obedience.

There is no test they take or class they attend to help establish their readiness. We simply leave it up to parents to decide when their young disciples are ready.

A Personal Response

My other response to this question is to share how Sally and I dealt with the issue for our two daughters. Our way is certainly not the only acceptable way to handle the issue. Other spiritually wise parents have handled it differently. Nevertheless, I commend our way to you for your consideration as you lay out a path for your children.

When our girls were small, we explained that they would be able to fully participate in the Lord's Supper sometime after they were 13. Admittedly, this response was somewhat arbitrary and sounds a bit legalistic—but it was a simple response that they could grasp, and it was enough to settle the issue for them. There were, however, important reasons why we encouraged them to wait.

1. **Wait for Understanding**—Probably the most compelling reason for us came out of 1 Corinthians 11:27-33 where Paul warns us of the perils of eating and drinking in an "unworthy manner." Though both of our girls confessed faith in Christ before their sixth birthdays, we wanted them to be old enough to contemplate the significance of the Lord's Supper. We wanted them to understand the meaning of the ordinance and have enough maturity to do the self-examination that Paul calls for in verse 28.

2. **Wait for More Independent Thinking**—We decided that they should come to the Lord's table after they were baptized, and we did not want them to be baptized before age 13. The main reason for this is that children are thinking more independently as they enter the teen years and therefore are more likely to embrace the decisions and commitments they make as their own. Our pre-teen decisions and commitments are often suspect in our minds as we get older. They are suspect in that we barely connect with the reason why we made the commitment. At age seven, I have a very vague memory of raising my hand in Sunday school and indicating a desire to follow Jesus. I remember sitting on the bed with my mom, praying, and writing the date of my conversion into my Bible. I am at a loss to tell you, however, what it was that was so compelling to me. I don't know if I understood what I was doing. I simply have no recollection now—neither did I have it when I was 13. Without that recollection, it was difficult to have confidence in the decision I made. This is probably why I felt a need to "accept Jesus into my heart" again during my teen years.

It is not uncommon for those who were baptized during their pre-teen years to feel a need to be "re-baptized" when they are older. Therefore, it made sense for us to encourage our children to hold off on baptism until a time when it would be more meaningful to them—when they could more fully embrace the commitment behind this public declaration of faith.

Although we do not believe baptism must necessarily precede participation in the Lord's Supper, it seemed more natural for our children to join the Lord at His table after they followed the Lord in the obedience of baptism. Since we planned for our girls to wait until at least age 13 to be baptized, it followed that they would also need to wait until then to take the Lord's Supper.

3. **Wait for Significance**—Even though our girls would have *qualified* for baptism and the Lord's Supper at an earlier age, we believe that waiting helped to impress on them the significance of these ordinances and the unspeakable privilege it is to participate in them.

4. **Wait for Anticipation**—Each time the tray passed them by, they could look forward to the day when they would join in this celebration. I believe that this period of anticipation made their first and subsequent experiences at the table sweeter and more meaningful to them.

5. **Wait for Memories**—We wanted our girls to remember their first experience at the Lord's table. Memories of the first decade of our lives are often fuzzy at best. Therefore, it made sense for them to wait until a time when they would more likely remember the experience.

6. **Wait for Maturity**—There is nothing particularly significant about age 13. We could have easily picked age 11, 12, or 14. Sally and I simply wanted to draw a very clear line for our girls that would mark a definite transition out of childhood into young adulthood. As arbitrary as it may seem, we saw tremendous value in having a tangible point where we began to place certain expectations and to offer certain privileges that are associated with maturity.

7. **Wait for Baptism**—It has been the historic position within many branches of the church that baptism should precede participation in this Lord's Supper. This position reflects the wisdom of welcoming a young person to the Lord's table after (rather than before) he has publicly confessed faith in Christ and followed Him in the obedience of baptism.

Even though we may ask our children to wait for a season before they fully participate in the Lord's Supper, the celebration can still be a significant experience for them in their pre-teen years. We should not wait to teach them about the meaning and importance of the table and how to examine themselves, confess their sins, and to remember the Lord's death until He comes.

It is my aim and earnest prayer that our children will know sweet fellowship with the living Christ and experience His life-changing, soul-satisfying work in their hearts. May the Lord use our efforts in preparing our children for His table to nudge them into closer fellowship with Him

Frequently Asked Questions

When should my child be baptized?

The only biblical requirement for baptism is faith in Jesus Christ alone for forgiveness of sins and the fulfillment of all His promises, including eternal life. However, the elders recommend that young people wait until at least age 11 before considering baptism—not because we doubt that a young child can be truly born again but because of a larger discipleship strategy that we have for young people in the church. Please see the "Concerning the Age for Baptism for Children: Reasons for Waiting" article in the appendix of the *Established in the Faith* booklet.)

I have more than one child who wants to be baptized. What do you recommend?

Assuming that the students being baptized are ready and sufficiently prepared, it is certainly acceptable for more than one student in a family to be baptized at the same time. However, there are some reasons why parents should consider preparing their students one at a time. A significant part of the preparation process involves at least six one-on-one sessions between parent and student. The purpose of this time is to discern the student's understanding and assurance of saving faith and his overall readiness for baptism. Many parents have appreciated being able to focus on one student at a time. Also, it is not uncommon for parents to discover during the preparation process that the candidate is not ready and should therefore wait to be baptized. Encouraging one student to wait becomes more difficult when another student in the family is ready. Parents in this situation often feel more pressure to proceed with the baptism of a student who should otherwise be encouraged to wait.

My child was baptized when he was a baby. Should he be baptized again?

Yes. The Bible teaches that baptism is for those who are trusting in Jesus Christ alone for the forgiveness of their sins and for the fulfillment of all His promises, including eternal life (Acts 2:41;

Acts 8:12; Acts 10:47–48). Therefore, we recommend that children wait until sometime after age 11 when they are able to understand, and we are confident that they are wholeheartedly embracing the gospel and committed to passionately follow Jesus Christ.

After my student is baptized, is he automatically a member of the church?

Yes and no! Yes, because in Christ "we [are] all baptized into one body" (1 Corinthians 12:13). That "body" is the Church. Our church is a local expression of Christ's Church, which has members and a membership process, which we encourage young people to pursue after baptism.

Who decides if my student is ready to be baptized?

Ultimately, the elders are responsible for all things related to baptism at the church, and thus final approval of all candidates for baptisms rests with the elders. The final step in the preparation process for young people is an interview with at least one elder who confirms the candidate's readiness for baptism. However, we view this preparation as a partnership with parents, and the process is designed to help parents be the first to discern if their student is ready or not.

I am a single parent. Is my former spouse expected to be involved?

The simple answer to this question is "let's talk" since the specific circumstances can vary from family to family. However, there are two priorities that can help to inform this decision. The first priority is that any parent who is involved must be a faithful follower of Jesus Christ. The second priority is that the parent should have spiritual interest and influence in the young person's life and faith. The preparation process is designed to launch what we hope will be an ongoing conversation about the life of faith and involvement in the discipleship of the young person. Please contact us if you would like to arrange for one of our elders to understand your situation and explore possibilities with you.

If I attended the parent orientation for one child, do I need to attend it again for my second child?

Once you attend a parent orientation, you are not required to attend it again for a second child. However, we are happy for parents to repeat the session if they would like to have a refresher before starting the process with another child. Also, the orientation provides an opportunity to connect with other parents at the church who are preparing their students at the same time.

How are parents involved in the baptism service?

This varies depending on the type of service and the family situation. Once a year, the church could have a special youth baptism service in which parents are more involved than they would be in a regular service. In most baptism services, parents are often standing with their children at the water's edge and are prepared to receive them with a towel after the baptism.

Can anyone baptize my child?

Although there are exceptions, generally baptisms are officiated by a pastor/elder of the church.

Is it okay to plan a private baptism service for my child in a location other than the church?

Although there are exceptions, we encourage candidates to be baptized in one of the public services of the church. The Apostle Paul reminds us that "we [are] all baptized into one body" (1 Corinthians 12:13). That "body" is the Church, and our church is the local expression of Christ's Church. Therefore, it makes the most sense for people to be baptized in the context of their local church community. Please contact us if you would like to explore other possibilities with one of our elders/pastors.

Other Questions?

For more information please contact: [name of children's ministry assistant]

YOUTH BAPTISM INTERVIEW TEAM PACKET

Preparation for the Baptism/Member Interview: Interview Team Letter

To: Team Members Interviewing Students for Youth Baptism and Membership

Thanks for taking the time to interview one or more of the students for baptism and membership. We greatly appreciate your willingness to be a part of this process.

Each interview team includes

- an **elder** who will preside over the interview,
- an **adult youth leader** who will be able to help with the interview and help follow up on anything that may come up in the interview,
- and, *when available,* an **older youth** who is perhaps the closest to the student in age and the baptism experience. I am hoping that this person will, possibly, more easily identify with the student and be an encouragement and support for him during the interview, as well as after.

All three team members should feel the freedom to ask questions of the student. I have suggested a general line of questioning, but feel free to adjust and adapt as needed.

Background: In preparation for baptism and membership, each student has had several sessions with a mentor (in most cases, a parent). During these sessions, the mentor was encouraged to review and make sure the student understands the gospel, emphasize his personal accountability before God, assess his assurance of salvation, review the meaning of baptism, and help him prepare his testimony. At one point in this preparation process, the student was encouraged to decisively affirm (or reaffirm) his faith in Christ and declare his intention to follow Him in obedience. If you would like to see the material the mentors used, let me know and I will see that you get it.

Following these private sessions, the student and mentor spent several hours in a youth baptism/membership preparation class with the other students and mentors who are preparing for baptism/membership. We reviewed the meaning of baptism and conducted a modified version of the "Ask Class," [a membership class] carefully covering the church covenant, the relational commitments, and the history of the church. Each of the students also gave his testimony. The Articles of Faith and Elder Affirmation of Faith were touched on briefly.

ELDERS, PLEASE MAKE SURE YOU REVIEW THE MATERIAL WE SENT YOU BEFORE YOU CONDUCT THE INTERVIEW.

At the conclusion of the youth baptism/membership preparation class, both the student and mentor completed **response forms.** These forms basically confirm their mutual desire for the student to move forward with baptism and possibly church membership. **You may want to arrive a few minutes early to read those forms.** They will be in the interview file folder in (or outside) the designated meeting room.

If you have any questions or want to discuss the interview further, please do not hesitate to contact [name and contact info] for scheduling details and any other questions or concerns you may have.

For the Joy of the Next Generation,

David Michael

YOUTH BAPTISM INTERVIEW TEAM PACKET

Suggested Questions for Youth Baptism/Membership Interview

- If you do not know the student well, ask a few questions to help you get to know the young person and his family a little better.
- Ask the student to share his feelings about the preparation time with the mentor. Were there any new insights or something about that time that made it particularly significant for him?
- Ask the student to describe his understanding of the gospel. What did God do to make his salvation possible?

  Note: This is a very important question. You are looking for evidence that the student both understands the gospel (mind) and embraces it (heart/affections). We have included with the elder packet an *Established in the Faith* booklet with the gospel section bookmarked. Mentors were instructed to make sure the student clearly understands and can articulate the gospel.)

  Some students may feel more secure reading a prepared testimony. If they do, you will still need to go beyond what they read on a prepared statement and engage them in conversation to discern their understanding.

- Ask the student to share some details about how he came to faith.
- Faith is expressed in word and deed, so it is important to explore the student's current walk with the Lord. Perhaps you could ask if there have been times recently when the young person felt particularly close to the Lord. You might ask if there are new things that the student is discovering about the Lord or if the student senses the Lord teaching him something in particular. You might inquire about regular times he has with the Lord.
- Explore the student's understanding of baptism and make sure he understands its meaning and significance. Also included in the elder packet is a summary of key points.
- Remind the student of the three questions that will be asked of him at the baptism service:

- *Are you now trusting in Jesus Christ alone for the forgiveness of your sins and for the fulfillment of all His promises to you, even eternal life?* (Make sure the student understands the question and ask if he is prepared to say yes to this question).

- *Do you now renounce Satan in all his works and all his ways?* (Make sure the student understands the question and ask if he is prepared to say yes to this question).

- *Do you intend, with God's help, to obey Jesus' teachings and to follow Him as your Lord?* (Make sure the student understands the question and ask if he is prepared to say yes to this question).

- Ask about the student's involvement in the church. Who are his closest friends? Who encourages the young person most in his faith? What gifts does the student believe he has? How are/might those gifts be used in the church?

- If the student is pursuing church membership, make sure he is familiar with, understands, and is ready to embrace the church covenant and the relational commitments document as a member of the church. You may want to spot-check the student's understanding of these documents by asking for an explanation of some selected points.

- Ask if the student has any questions for you.

- If you feel the student is ready to move ahead, describe the next steps and make sure he is aware of the baptism and covenant affirmation dates (information below).

- After the student is excused, please take a few minutes to discuss the interview and complete the interview form. If there are any concerns that you have, please note them on the form or contact [pastor's name]. We are especially interested in any specific areas where growth or further understanding is needed.

YOUTH BAPTISM INTERVIEW TEAM PACKET
Essential Elements of the Gospel

There are four essential elements that the student will need to understand and be able to put into words.

1. **Truth About God**

   A. **God is holy.**

   - **He does not sin, do evil, or make mistakes.**

     God is not man, that he should lie, or a son of man, that he should change his mind... (Numbers 23:19a)

     ...God cannot be tempted with evil, and he himself tempts no one. (James 1:13b)

   - **God is separated from sin.**

     Holiness is more than *not sinning*. To be holy is to be completely separated from sin. Sin and holiness cannot be in the same place. When Adam and Eve sinned, they hid from the presence of the Lord. The Holy of Holies in the tabernacle and temple reminded Israel that God was separated from them because He was holy.

   - **Because God is holy, we must be holy, too.**

     "Speak to all the congregation of the people of Israel and say to them, You shall be holy, for I the LORD your God am holy."(Leviticus 19:2)

     Strive for peace with everyone, and for the holiness without which no one will see the Lord. (Hebrews 12:14)

     but as he who called you is holy, you also be holy in all your conduct, ¹⁶since it is written, "You shall be holy, for I am holy." (1 Peter 1:15-16)

B. **God is devoted to His glory.**

- **Everything God has done, and all that He is doing and all that He ever will do is for His glory and His glory alone.**

  He has compassion on His people so that *"Nations will fear the name of the LORD, and all the kings of the earth will fear [His] glory." (Psalm 102:15)*

  He restrained His hand from Pharaoh *"to show you [His] power, so that [His] name may be proclaimed in all the earth." (Exodus 9:16)*

  Jesus came for the glory of God (John 17:5).

  Jesus healed for the glory of God (John 11:4).

  Jesus prayed for the glory of God (John 17:24).

  In the end (God's goal): *...the earth will be filled with the knowledge of the glory of the LORD... (Habakkuk 2:14)*

  ...from the rising of the sun, to its setting [His] name will be great among the nations... (Malachi 1:11)

- **God created (made) us for His glory.**

  "...bring my sons from afar and my daughters from the end of the earth...whom I created for my glory..." (Isaiah 43:6b-7a)

- **Because we were made for God's glory, we must live for His glory.**

  So, whether you eat or drink, or whatever you do, do all to the glory of God. (1 Corinthians 10:31)

2. **Truth About Sin**

   A. **Because of Adam's sin, we all, as human beings, are born in sin—we have a corrupt nature, which means we are born sinful.**

   Therefore, just as sin came into the world through one man, and death through sin, and so death spread to all men because all sinned— (Romans 5:12)

B. **Because of our sin, we have failed to please God.**

For the mind that is set on the flesh is hostile to God, for it does not submit to God's law; indeed, it cannot. ⁸Those who are in the flesh cannot please God. (Romans 8:7-8)

- **We have failed to be holy.**

  "None is righteous, ¹¹no, not one; no one understands; no one seeks for God. ¹²All have turned aside; together they have become worthless; no one does good, not even one." (Romans 3:10-12)

- **We have failed to live for His glory.**

  for all have sinned and fall short of the glory of God, (Romans 3:23)

- We don't love Him like we should. We don't trust Him like we should. We don't treasure Him like we should, etc.

C. **Because of our sin, God is very angry with us.**

But because of your hard and impenitent heart you are storing up wrath for yourself on the day of wrath when God's righteous judgment will be revealed. (Romans 2:5)

And you were dead in the trespasses and sins....³...and were by nature children of wrath, like the rest of mankind. (Ephesians 2:1a, 3b)

D. **Because of our sin, we are condemned to hell.**

"Whoever believes in him is not condemned, but whoever does not believe is condemned already, because he has not believed in the name of the only Son of God." (John 3:18)

"Then the king said to the attendants, 'Bind him hand and foot and cast him into the outer darkness. In that place there will be weeping and gnashing of teeth.'" (Matthew 22:13)

3. **Truth About What Christ Did**

The main point to emphasize is that Christ is our substitute. He took our place. He bore (carried) our sins instead of us. He became the object of God's wrath instead of us. He died instead of us.

A. **Christ bore our sins.**

He himself bore our sins in his body on the tree, that we might die to sin and live to righteousness. By his wounds you have been healed. (1 Peter 2:24)

For I delivered to you as of first importance what I also received: that Christ died for our sins in accordance with the Scriptures, (1 Corinthians 15:3)

B. **Christ became a curse for us.**

Christ redeemed us from the curse of the law by becoming a curse for us—for it is written, "Cursed is everyone who is hanged on a tree"— (Galatians 3:13)

C. **Christ became our righteousness.**

- **In Christ we can be holy.**

   For our sake he made him to be sin who knew no sin, so that in him we might become the righteousness of God. (2 Corinthians 5:21)

   For as by the one man's disobedience the many were made sinners, so by the one man's obedience the many will be made righteous. (Romans 5:19)

- **In Christ we glorify God.**

   "All mine are yours, and yours are mine, and I am glorified in them." (John 17:10)

   ..."Now is the Son of Man glorified, and God is glorified in him." (John 13:31b)

4. **Truth About Faith**

   A. **Faith is the way we benefit from what Jesus did for us.**

   For by grace you have been saved through faith. (Ephesians 2:8a)

   B. **Faith is not something we do; it is a gift of God.**

   And this is not your own doing; it is the gift of God, not a result of works, so that no one may boast. (Ephesians 2:8b-9)

C. **Faith is trusting in Christ ALONE for the forgiveness of our sins and the fulfillment of all His promises to us.**

But when the goodness and loving kindness of God our Savior appeared, [5]he saved us, not because of works done by us in righteousness, but according to his own mercy, by the washing of regeneration and renewal of the Holy Spirit, [6]whom he poured out on us richly through Jesus Christ our Savior, [7]so that being justified by his grace we might become heirs according to the hope of eternal life. (Titus 3:4-7)

D. **Faith is treasuring Christ.**

"Do not lay up for yourselves treasures on earth, where moth and rust destroy and where thieves break in and steal, [20]but lay up for yourselves treasures in heaven, where neither moth nor rust destroys and where thieves do not break in and steal. [21]For where your treasure is, there your heart will be also." (Matthew 6:19-21)

"The kingdom of heaven is like treasure hidden in a field, which a man found and covered up. Then in his joy he goes and sells all that he has and buys that field. [45]Again, the kingdom of heaven is like a merchant in search of fine pearls, [46]who, on finding one pearl of great value, went and sold all that he had and bought it." (Matthew 13:44-46)

"But God said to him, 'Fool! This night your soul is required of you, and the things you have prepared, whose will they be?' [21]So is the one who lays up treasure for himself and is not rich toward God." (Luke 12:20-21)

Treasuring Christ Together

We want the student to understand the gospel and be able to communicate it in a coherent and personal way. However, the ability to know, understand, and articulate the gospel does not necessarily point to authentic faith. A young person can memorize the elements of the gospel and the supporting texts without ever treasuring Christ as his own.

YOUTH BAPTISM INTERVIEW TEAM PACKET
The Meaning of Baptism

What is Baptism?

1. **Baptism is immersion into water.**

   This is the basic meaning of the word "baptism," but for the Christian its meaning is much richer and deeper.

2. **Baptism is a symbol.**
   A. **The Death and Resurrection of Jesus**
   B. **What God Has Accomplished**

   Baptism is a symbol of the spiritual change that God has worked in our lives. It is a transition from spiritual and eternal death to spiritual and eternal life. It is moving from hopelessness into hopefulness, from darkness into light, and from slavery to sin to freedom in Christ. In baptism, we symbolically express our acceptance of death with Christ, putting an end to our old way of life and rising with Christ to begin a new kind of life in Him.

   C. **Washing/Cleansing from Sin**
   D. **Entrance into the Body of Christ, the Church**

3. **Baptism is an act of obedience to the Lord's command and following His example.**

4. **Baptism is a public declaration of faith in Jesus Christ.**

   In baptism, we express with our whole body our heart's acceptance of Christ's Lordship. Becoming a Christian involves the body as well as the heart. In conversion, the heart is freed from slavery to sin to be enslaved to God.

5. **Baptism is a blessing.**

   The student should understand by now that baptism does not accomplish our salvation, but he should not miss the great blessing in the baptism experience.

Pastor/Elder Questions and Response for the Baptism Service

Baptismal questions asked by the pastor/elder to the student in the water of baptism.

Question: Are you now trusting in Jesus Christ alone for the forgiveness of your sins and for the fulfillment of all His promises to you, even eternal life?

Answer: I am.

Question: Do you now renounce Satan in all his works and all his ways?

Answer: I do.

Question: Do you intend, with God's help, to obey Jesus' teachings and to follow Him as your Lord?

Answer: I do.

Pastoral Response just before immersion: Upon your profession of faith in Jesus Christ as your Savior and Lord, and in obedience to His command, I now baptize you in the name of the Father and of the Son and of the Holy Spirit.

Truth:78

Our vision is that the next generations may know, honor, and treasure God, setting their hope in Christ alone, so that they will live as faithful disciples for the glory of God.

It is our mission to inspire and equip the church and home for the comprehensive discipleship of the next generation. To that end, we develop resources that put God at the center, focus on the gospel, and exalt Christ. They are grounded in sound doctrine for faithful discipleship.

Resources and Training Materials

Curriculum

We publish materials for formal Bible instruction in the classroom including Sunday School, Midweek Bible programs, Backyard Bible Clubs/VBS, and multi-age studies. The scope and sequence reflect our commitment to teach children and youth the whole counsel of God over the course of their education. Most materials can easily be adapted for use in Christian schools and homeschools.

Vision-Casting and Training

We offer a wide variety of booklets, video and audio seminars, articles, and other practical training resources designed to assist ministry leaders, volunteers, and parents to implement Truth78's vision and mission in their churches and homes. Many are available for free at Truth78.org.

Parenting and Family Discipleship

Truth78 equips parents to disciple their children with booklets, video presentations, family devotionals, children's books, articles, apps, and more. Curricula include take-home pages to help parents nurture faith at home by applying classroom lessons to their child's daily experience.

Bible Memory

Truth78 publishes Fighter Verses, the collection of 260 passages uniquely suited to arm individuals, families, and whole churches for the fight of faith. Companion resources include study guides, journals, coloring books, and songs to encourage Scripture memory, as well as Foundation Verses to help toddlers and preschoolers lay a firm biblical foundation.

For more information about resources and services, please contact us:

Truth78.org • info@Truth78.org
(877) 400-1414

Zealous

Vision and framework for the discipleship of the next generation.

The next generation needs parents, teachers, and church leaders who are zealous for their discipleship. But where does zeal come from and what does it look like day today?

In *Zealous*, long-time pastor and Truth78 Executive Director, David Michael describes a fervor and diligence born out of a passion for God and His glory and presents seven commitments that provide a vision and framework for your discipleship of the next generation...so that they might set their hope in God (Psalm 78:1-8).

Truth78.org/zealous

A Guide to Growing Zeal for the Discipleship of the Next Generations

Apply the 7 commitments in your church and home

How can you make a vision for the discipleship of the next generations a reality for the children and youth growing up in your home and church? This guide offers practical application of the vision and framework presented in *Zealous*. Find next-step opportunities for each of the seven commitments for children's discipleship in this free PDF.

Truth78.org/grow-zeal

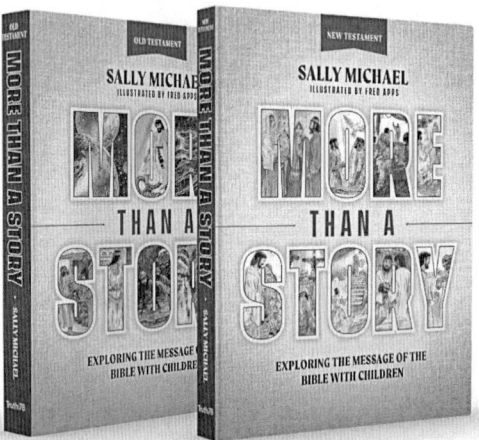

More Than a Story

Introduce children to a glorious God.

More Than a Story takes children (ages 6-12) on a chronological journey through the Bible with a God-centered, gospel-focused, discipleship-oriented, theologically grounded perspective.

Old Testament and New Testament volumes are available individually or as a bundle.

Truth78.org/more-than-a-story

Making HIM Known books

A series of books to teach children about the character and worth of God.

These illustrated family devotionals provide a way for the entire family to learn about our great God and His Word. Each chapter of these read-to and read-along books for elementary-age children ends with personal application and activities and is enhanced by full-color illustrations.

Each book is adapted from a Truth78 curriculum.

Truth78.org/making-him-known-series

GROWING IN THE WORD SERIES

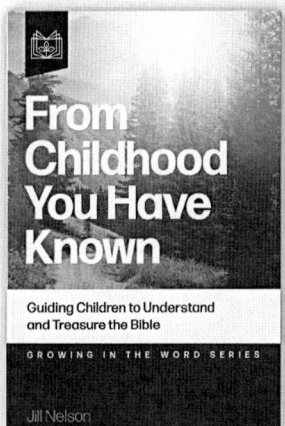
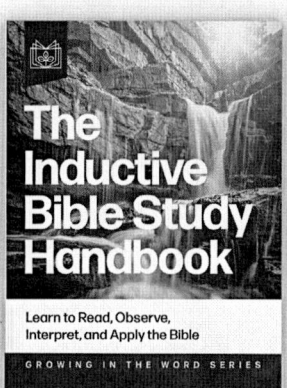
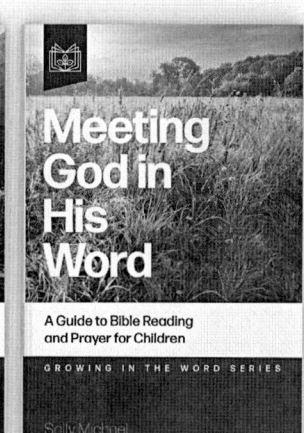

God has given us in the Bible a book like no other, and we have been given the great responsibility and privilege to pass its life-giving truth to the next generation. The Growing in the Word Series aims to inspire and equip the church and home to teach the next generation to read and study the Bible, pray for understanding and a right heart, and apply what they learn to their daily lives.

Resources in this series provide an introduction to the Bible, its message, and use; a reading plan; help with Bible memory and Scripture-focused prayer; age-appropriate training toward biblical literacy; and inductive Bible study tools to help children and youth learn to read, observe, interpret, and apply the Bible to their everyday lives.

Help the children and youth in your home and church come to know and love God's Word and, more importantly, the God who reveals Himself through His Word. Their very life and eternal joy depend upon it!

The following booklets are included in the Growing in the Word Series:

- **From Childhood You Have Known:**
  Guiding Children to Understand and Treasure the Bible
- **The Inductive Bible Study Handbook:**
  Learn to Read, Observe, Interpret, and Apply the Bible
- **Meeting God in His Word:**
  A Guide to Bible Reading and Prayer for Children